SpringerBriefs in Digital Spaces

For further volumes:
http://www.springer.com/series/10461

Namjae Cho

The Use of Smart Mobile Equipment for the Innovation in Organizational Coordination

 Springer

Namjae Cho
School of Management
Hanyang University
Seoul
Republic of Korea (South Korea)

ISSN 2193-5890   ISSN 2193-5904   (electronic)
ISBN 978-3-642-30846-8 ISBN 978-3-642-30847-5   (eBook)
DOI 10.1007/978-3-642-30847-5
Springer Heidelberg New York Dordrecht London

Library of Congress Control Number: 2012940462

Printed on acid-free paper

Springer is part of Springer Science+Business Media (www.springer.com)

Summary

Recent increases in uncertainty and speed of market change are driving the adoption of new intelligent mobile office systems. Organizational information systems paradigm suggests that a right match between organizational character-istics and the use of technology is critical in producing desired results. Following such perspective this study focused on the relationship between task characteristics and the use of mobile office systems with an intention to find out factors that affect the adoption of modern mobile office systems. The research results show that in performing tasks with high mobility users tend to use extensive mobile office functions. When the task has a high level of interdependency with external busi-ness partners, users relied on specialized mobile functions such as FFA, SFA and ERP. Highly volatile environment with many unexpected task changes caused an extensive use of task specific functions that help to solve problems at hand. Further, analyses of the differences of mobile office use by department showed that sales department used more communication functions than others, while admin-istrative departments rely more on such task specific functions as mobile CRM and KM than others. Additional case study shows how the application of new technology the effectiveness of organizational coordination. Based on the research the concept of convergent coordination is suggested as well as the direction for future research.

Keywords Organizational information process paradigm · Task complexity · Task interdependence · Task variability · Task mobility · Mobile office system

v

Acknowledgments

The completion of this booklet is accomplished with the help of several individuals and organizations.

I would like to express my appreciation to my research assistants. Ms. Ji Youn Kim helped to collect and analyze survey data on the use of mobile office systems. Ms. Joung In Choi helped me to complete the case study on the development and use of mobile office systems in Seoul Metropolitan Railway Transit Company.

My thanks should also go to the managers of SMRT for allowing to perform the case study and to the managers of many Korean companies including Samsung and KT for the collection of survey data.

Most of all, Professor Ahmed Bounfour of University of Paris Sud supported and encouraged the pursuit of this research. My debt also goes to Korea Information Society Development Institute for their provision of supports and comments.

Contents

**The Use of Smart Mobile Equipment for the Innovation
in Organizational Coordination** 1
1 Introduction 1
2 Theoretical Background and Research Hypotheses 3
  2.1 Mobile Office System 3
  2.2 Technology and Coordination: Organizational
      Information Processing Theory View.................... 8
  2.3 Task Characteristics and Research Hypotheses 12
3 Research Method.. 17
  3.1 Research Model................................... 17
  3.2 Operational Definition of Variables.................... 17
  3.3 Data Collection 18
4 Results of Data Analysis 20
  4.1 General Characteristics of the Sample 20
  4.2 Test of Research Instruments 20
  4.3 Revision of Research Model and Hypotheses 22
  4.4 Test of Hypotheses 23
5 Case Study of the Use of Mobile Office 25
  5.1 Background of the Case Study 25
  5.2 Adoption of Mobile Office System at SMRT 27
  5.3 Characteristics of the Mobile Office System of SMRT 29
  5.4 Effect of the Adoption of Mobile Office System
      at SMRT 31
6 Conclusion.. 32
References... 34

The Use of Smart Mobile Equipment for the Innovation in Organizational Coordination

1 Introduction

There is a series of emerging information technologies that have a good potential to enable emergent business innovation. Most of all, the new smart phone is an offspring of digital convergence of network, media, and electronic equipments. Smart phone, being an enabler of telecommunications network and open internet network access, help business people use diverse modes of data, information, images, and video on a unified mobile application platform. One major impact of such convergence is the increase of innovation potential in the structure and process of organizational coordination.

The importance of coordination in the process of creating value in organizations has been emphasized repeatedly (Argyres 1999; Malone and Crowston 1994; Gittell and Weiss 2004). Coordination is considered as the core principle of organizing (Faraj and Xiao 2006; Malone and Crowston 1994). Coordination can be considered as an umbrella concept which include integration (combining to an integral whole), collaboration (working jointly), and cooperation (joint operation). It is reported that an effective coordination contribute to organizational decision making, business performance, cost saving, flexible response to the changes in market (Ballou et al. 2000; Hoyt and Huq 2000; Barratt 2004; Ding and Chen 2008).

Due to the complexity of coordination, diverse factors affect the approaches, process, and outcome of coordination. For example, the focus and goals of coordination is affected by the nature of product. When the product is stable, it is advised to focus on the reduction of cost. On the other hand, when the product has a dynamic nature, the focus of management will be directed toward the fast development of new products, swift incorporation of new technology, and the implementation of new innovation.

At the core of the coordination of business activities lies the efficient and effective sharing of information using new technologies. Sharing information

N. Cho, *The Use of Smart Mobile Equipment for the Innovation in Organizational Coordination*, SpringerBriefs in Digital Spaces, DOI: 10.1007/978-3-642-30847-5_1,
© The Author(s) 2013

could be realized through the adoption of standard data codes and information interchange technologies. However, the more difficult problem in the implementation of information sharing and coordination than the adoption of technology is the coordination of culture and business practices.

This project is to explore the potential of the use of new convergence technology, e.g. smart mobile phones, for an innovation in organizational productivity. A few companies like Samsung Insurance, Kolong, and Green Cross in Korea recently launched new IT projects to extend their corporate information systems to the use of smart phones so that their employees can access and share organizational information stored in the legacy system, intranets, and knowledge management systems. These attempts are expected to change the way people work and perform business activities. We will perform comparative case studies of these companies so that we can better understand how different business contexts affect the use of this new technology for the improvements in organizational coordination. In addition we plan to perform a survey to analyze organizational and individual responses to this new business practices.

The importance of organizations' information management process increases as it is directly related to the survival of companies under hyper-turbulent business environment. One critical capacity required for modern companies under rapidly changing industrial environment is the establishment of information management systems that help managers understand and interpret business environment correctly and respond quickly to the changes. For such reasons real-time information communication within and across organizational boundary is considered critical as a strategic infrastructure. Enhanced information processing capacity not only improves operational efficiency and corporate competitiveness, but it also helps companies capture new business opportunities for growth through efficient and effective decision making.

Mobile office systems have recently become the focus of interest as a key information processing technology as a stable wireless network environment for mobile Internet is secured and as powerful mobile equipment such smart phone is widely available. Mobile office system is considered to provide a task environment that enables the use of information anytime and anywhere using portable computers, mobile phones, and PDAs. It can also be integrated to business processes so that right business tools can be used for under appropriate situations (KT Economic Research Center 2010).

The adoption of mobile office environment started to spread out in Korea with the initiative of large corporations and public sector. The mobile office system is expected to provide the 'smartness' required for modern organizations as well as the 'mobility' required to cope with rapid changes.

The effect of the use of a technology is optimized when the technology is designed and applied to match the contingency of an organization. In this vein the organizational demand for technological functionalities should be carefully studied to guide a successful adoption of a new technology. However, systematic and empirical research around the use of mobile office system is yet far from sufficient.

This research is aimed to examine the nature of task characteristics and its relationship to the use of mobile office systems in order to understand the appropriate context of the use of mobile office system within an organization from the perspective of task-technology fit theory.

2 Theoretical Background and Research Hypotheses

2.1 Mobile Office System

2.1.1 Nature of Mobile Office System

Mobile Office System is an enterprise information technology which uses portable terminals to access corporate information systems to manage data and human resources in remote locations (Gebauer and Shaw 2004). Mobile office is being diffused rapidly as its adoption enables efficient task processing by employees working inside and outside of the office as well as in the operational field. Mobile office emerged as notebook computers are introduced as an important source of corporate competitiveness based on their high level of mobility. PDAs (Personal Digital Assistance) are also used as a hand-held terminal for mobile office for the management of inventory in logistics and retailing function based on wireless technology such as IrDA. The scope of today's Mobile Office System usage includes real-time task processing using groupware, corporate bulletin board, task schedule manager, ERP, SCM, CRM, and Intranets.

The introduction of Mobile Office System enables activity-centric and user-centric task processing as corporate data can be used anytime anywhere to improve productivity through improved communication and collaboration among employees (Beulen and Streng 2002). The effect of the use of Mobile Office System is considered to include fast decision making, reduction of operating costs, improved speed of service, improved organizational task efficiency, improved productivity, and increased level of customer service. The use of mobile office is expanding from logistics, retail, service, and insurance industries into such sectors as education, healthcare and public services.

2.1.2 Status of Mobile Office Adoption in Korea

Mobile office based on specialized PDA has long been used in Korea in various industries. Such systems largely used for field task management and sales resource management. The improvements in ubiquitous technology environment and safety infrastructure for high-speed mobile network enabled the convenient use of advanced smart phones for mobile office. Mobile office based on smart phone has high-level of interconnectivity and portability compared to PDSs and Laptops.

For this reason, smart phone-based mobile office is being actively adopted by companies in different sizes as well as public sector organizations.

The number of mobile office users is expected to increase from about 10,000 in 2009 to 1,000,000 by 2012. (Broadcasting and Communications Council 2010). Mobile office system is being actively adopted within Korea. KT (Korea Telecom) Economic Research (2010) reported that investment into mobile office environment in 2009 was 2.9 Trillion KRW and is expected to grow rapidly to reach 5.9 Trillion KRW by 2014.

Large Korean conglomerates such as Samsung, Kolon, and SK and large companies such as KT (Korea Telecom) and POSCO adopted corporate-wide mobile office systems. For example, Samsung group used smart phones for approval, e-mail, and employee search. Kolon group provided smart phone with mobile office to 8,000 employees of its 42 subsidiaries. SK Group spreads out a customized mobile office throughout its subsidiaries. Dongbu group uses mobile office for approval, pursues improvements in task process and corporate culture, and is planning to expand the system to sales and inventory management functions. POSCO provided smart phones to all managers for the use of e-mail, marketing-related tasks, and e-learning services. Shinhan Bank provides smart phones to 1,000 executive managers and had them use it for document approval, employee search, decision making, and messaging.

The adoption of smart phones for mobile office can also be observed in public sector. Ministry of Internal Administration and Safety provided smart phones connected to mobile office to 3,000 managers for the purpose of approval, reporting, and e-mail and is pursuing the adoption of extended standard for inter-operation. Broadcasting bureau uses smart phones with a connection to Internet phone exchange, FMC services, and weather-related service operator systems. Seoul Metropolitan Transit Railway, a public company owned and operated by the city of Seoul, uses mobile office with smart phones for real-time facility testing and maintenance, technical problem reporting, and the reporting of corresponding responses, as well as unified group communication functions. Table 1a, b enumerate organizations that adopt mobile office systems by the time of December, 2010.

2.1.3 Mobile Office System Functions

Mobile office service under mobile office system environment implies that corporate business tasks are performed using Laptops, PDAs, and smart phones as well as Internet services based on desktop computers to enable continuous access to enterprise information systems anytime anywhere. EMS (Enterprise Mobility Service) should include mobile equipment, mobile solutions, and related network infrastructure. The establishment of EMS should consider unique business context of each companies. The adoption of EMS is expected to help reduce communication cost and improve task efficiency so that RTE (Real Time Enterprise) can be realized.

Mobile office functions provided through EMS environment can be divided into two groups: primary functions related to company groupware and specialized

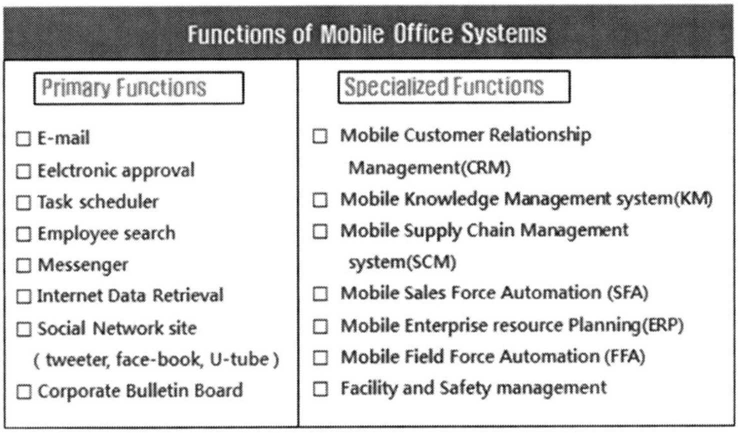

Fig. 1 Classification of Mobile Office Functions

functions to process specific tasks inter-operated with corporate legacy information systems as summarized in Fig. 1.

2.1.4 Mobile Office System Primary Functions

Mobile office system primary functions are provided via the interconnection with company groupware. These functions include the followings:

- **e-mail:** remote use of company e-mail server
- **Electronic approval:** real-time decision making and tracking using mobile electronic approval service which also provide review of related documents and opinions.
- **Task scheduler:** registration and search of task schedules using mobile terminals
- **Employee search:** registration and search of employee information, directory, and organization chart using mobile terminals which also allow immediate communication, messaging, and mailing.
- **Messenger:** coordinate task opinions and support fast decision making via the use of company messenger services among organizational members
- **Internet Data Retrieval:** search task-related information via Internet portals and enterprise databases
- **Social Network service:** real-time access to social network services for interaction among organizational members
- **Corporate Bulletin Board:** registration and search of task ideas and opinions using corporate groupware

Table 1 Mobile office adoption in Korea (2010. 12) **(a)**, Mobile office adoption in Korea (2010. 12)

Type	Organization	Focus of scope	Characteristics
(a) Smart Phone-based mobile office systems			
Corporate-wide adoption	Amore pacific (cosmetic)	Sales support, customer management	Commonly used functions
	Seoul metro railway	Operational information	• e-mail, electronic approval, groupware functions
	Asan hospital	Patient list, test results	• Sales support and field operation support
	Shinyoung security	Customer relationship	• Rapid customer responses support
	Pharmaceutics: green cross, Hanmi, Ankook, Kyungnam, Daewoong	Sales support, inventory inquiry, order processing, approval, data search	• Field collaboration support
	Daewoo construction	Field collaboration	• Interconnection with legacy information system
	Cheongjungwon food	Groupware, sales information, ERP	• Data retrieval and search
	Ministry of Admin.	Approval, admin service	
	Broadcasting bureau	Weather related services	
	IBM Korea	Unified communication, groupware service	
	Mirae asset, Hana investment, Daewoo secutries, Samsung secutries	Customer information, transaction information, approvall, e-mail function home trading	
Corporate groups	Samsung, Hyundai, CJ, KT, Samyang, Kolon, Lotte, POSCO, Dongbu, Hyosung, Kumho-Asiana	Groupware, specialized tasks	Rolling out from group HQ and central subsidiaries to other related companies
Basic	Korean air, Aanjin, Deloite KCC, MK trend,	E-mail, approval	Conservative culture

(continued)

Table 1 (continued)

Type	Organization	Scope	Characteristics
(b) PDA-based mobile office systems			
Specialized PDA	Chungang hospital, Samsung medical	Prescription, electronic charts	Real-time collection and retrieval of medical information
	Patent bureau, local governments	Mobile tax processing	
	Agricultural Products Distribution Co.	Mobile price search	
	LG electronics	Post-sales services	Enterprise CRM inter-operation
	Shilla hotel	Customer management	
	S1 Safety Service Co.	Safety service System	GPS function, central control system, real-time tracking
	Logistics companies: Daehan, Hanjin, Shinsegi, Post offices	Freight tracking	
	Inurance companies: Kumho, SK, Daehan	Mobile sales support	Customer management, field contract design processing
	LG retail, department of railway service	Mobile facility management	Facility check-ups, maintenance management
	Sampyo, Cheil Sugar, Nongshim, Korea red cross	Mobile sales and logistics support	Business processes: order, purchase, delivery, warehouse management, sales, payment
	SK Group	'SK mania' system	Wireless enterprise portal, Group intranet

2.1.5 Mobile Office System Specialized Functions

Specialized functions of mobile office systems include services which help perform specific business activities such as CRM, KM, SCM, SFA, FFA, and ERP.

- **Mobile Customer Relationship Management (CRM):** Mobile CRM emphasizes personalization, mobility, immediacy, location sensitivity, and continuity. Mobile CRM helps provide services and contents customized to individual customers whenever they want sensitive to the location of customers using corporate customer information base.
- **Mobile Sales Force Automation (SFA):** Mobile SFA system provide field sales people with customer contact information and product information. It helps process specification, order processing, and approval processing through the integration of sales, marketing, and customer service information.
- **Mobile** Enterprise Resource Planning **(ERP):** ERP help to integrate production, logistics, finance, accounting, sales, purchasing, and inventory management processes so that relevant information can be shared to facilitate business decision making and implementation. Mobile ERP interconnects with enterprise ERP systems to support people and processes in the field for optimal utilization of organizational resources.
- **Mobile Field Force Automation (FFA): Mobile** FFA is a wireless B2E solution to support field managers and workers to improve productivity and reduce costs of field activities via integrated middleware services, contents, and applications which provide such services as real-time work scheduling.
- **Mobile Knowledge Management System (MKM):** Knowledge management system focuses on the creation, collection, organization, and sharing of less-structured knowledge related to managerial activities in an organization (Alavi and Leidner 1999). Mobile knowledge management system help employees retrieve, refer, and use organizational knowledge base using personal mobile equipment.
- **Facility and Safety Management:** Mobile facility and safety management service helps checking facilities and performing safety maintenance tasks. It helps receive orders related to facility checking and maintenance and process appropriate tasks by reporting and getting approval without spatial and temporal limitations.

2.2 Technology and Coordination: Organizational Information Processing Theory View

Organization information processing paradigm suggests that best performance is the result of the match between organizational demand for information processing and technological supply of information processing capability. Galbraith (1977) viewed that the central function of an organization is the processing of information to cope with environmental uncertainty, which is considered as the difference between the amount of information required to perform a task and the amount of information actually provided. When appropriate amount of information is provided, the level of uncertainty decreases and thus, the performance of an organization increases.

Under high environmental uncertainty the elements of external environment are complex, and dynamically change making it difficult to expect. The complexity and dynamism are the two major dimensions of uncertainty and tend to be correlated in practice (Osborn and Hunt 1974; Yasai-Ardekani 1986). Organizational capability to process a large amount of information is considered critical to overcome environment uncertainty (Tushman and Nadler 1978). Tichy (1983) suggests that complex and rapidly changing environment creates incremental uncertainty which require increased information processing capability.

Researchers in this stream have focused on such organizational contingency variables as organizational characteristics, environmental characteristics, technological characteristics, task characteristics, and individual characteristics (Astley and Van de Ven 1981; Nadler and Tushman 1998; Weill and Olson 1989). Goodhue and Thompson (1995) specifically formalized the role of task-technology fit in producing high performance from the use of information technologies. They suggest that the fit between task characteristics (such as routineness and interdependence) and the nature of technology leads high level of utilization of the technology and increase in performance. Their model has been used to examine such technologies as e-commerce, group support systems, and web-based procurements.

Nature of a task is related to the nature of information required. For example, Gordon et al. (1976) explain differences in information characteristics required by tasks at each stage of strategic decision making. Routine and repetitive tasks require more internal, historical, periodic, detailed and specific information. As the level of difficulty and diversity of a task increases more external, futuristic, ad hoc, comprehensive, and integrative information is required. They suggest that the provision of information appropriate to the scope and goal of a task is the key to the accomplishment of high performance. Further, tasks with high level of exception and low level of analyzability tend to require compressed and composite information (Kirs et al. 1989). On the other hand, task with high level of diversity and low in analyzability tend to require broad scope of information (Ghani 1992). As an extension of this logic, the analysis of the relationship between organizational task characteristics and the use of mobile office system functions is expected to provide us with important implications for the successful design, adoption and use of modern mobile office systems.

Modern business environment is characterized by volatility and turbulence. Market demand continues to change over time due to the changes in customer preferences, new products introduced rapidly, increasing variety of products and functionality, global flow of goods and services, and worldwide swift exchange of information. Market dynamism refers to changes in demand and competition over time and market complexity implies the increase in the number of factors to be taken care of. Under such dynamic and complex environment managers cannot rely on intuition, good will, and visionary philosophy as guiding principle (Bonabeau 2003). The planning and implementation of supply network coordination needs systematic coordination mechanisms and analytical tools for operational calibration aligned to unique needs of a business environment.

In addition the tools and mechanisms of coordination should be designed to contribute not only to cost reduction but also to responsiveness, security, sustainability, resilience, and innovation (Melnyk et al. 2010).

The complexity of supply network environment is further heightened by interactions formerly unavailable or unrealized efficiently. These interactions are based on the exchange of information among suppliers and the sharing of knowledge among customers and consumers. However, the interaction among suppliers that influence the decision of individual supplier is only implicitly reflected in competitive market price. However, the interaction among suppliers will also affect the diffusion of new technologies and the adoption of new business practices.

In general the meaning of coordination as "managing dependencies between activities" is widely accepted (Malone and Crowston 1994). However, the concept of coordination lacks an agreed on structure as there are differences in the conceptualization of coordination (Archinder et al. 2008). In addition, as the scope and perspective of coordination evolve, the operational description of coordination also evolved over time. For this reason, for a more extensive future research on coordination, more empirical research is called for. A clarified model of coordination is needed to compare and integrate variations of the conceptualization of coordination.

Coordination within an organization or between organizations with transactional activities are supposed to be aligned together so that activities can flow seamlessly. Here, the exchange of information is intensive and repetitive and intimate relationships are formed. On the other hand, however, in much of the coordination and interaction in the supply network, the durations of contract are relatively short and the partners are changed from time to time or even in each contract.

Properties related to the substance of coordination involve the coerciveness, formality, and dynamism. When employed, these characteristics can be used for broadening our understandings on coordination. For example, from the perspective of coerciveness, coordination can be classified into voluntary, intrinsically motivated coordination and enforced, externally motivated coordination. This classification has a potential to provide us with a way to enrich our understanding of coordination process by incorporating the perspective of political economic paradigm to the formative analysis of collaboration process.

The use of information technology has been considered as one of the most influential coordination mechanism. For example, EDI(electronic document interchange) is the mostly employed and analyzed technology for inter-organizational coordination, and the use of internet is the most widely diffused mechanism for inter-organizational communication and transaction (Majchzak et al. 2000). Recent developments in information technologies provide promising potential to improve the efficiency and effectiveness of supply network coordination. For example, one major emergent technology of interest is the multimedia mobile terminal and smart phone.

An effective use of such rich information processing medium has the potential to accomplish desired coordination under highly uncertain and ambiguous business environment (Daft et al. 1987; Rice 1992; Cho et al. 2007). An effective sharing and exchange of information enabled by modern technologies can help companies to achieve improvements in cost, confidence, mutual trust, flexibility, and agility (Cachon and Fisher 2000; Kanawattanachai and Yoo 2007; Zhou and Benton 2007). Further, the information environment is experiencing a massive convergence of traditionally separate technologies such as telecommunications, computing, and broadcasting. This trend casts an unprecedentedly high capacity in the richness of the medium for information exchange. These convergence technologies can handle higher intensity of diverse mode of information such as images, voices, sounds, and motion compared to the traditional ones, which relied on texts and numbers.

Research should be performed to examine the relationship between the use of convergence media technology and the coordination within an organization and at the interface of network members. Analysis of early adopters of mobile office environment and mobile support systems to support purchasing, procurement, and sales function can help us to understand factors, logic, and issues that drive intra- and multi-echelon inter-organizational coordination. Existing research on the exchange of textual and numerical transaction information and its contribution to alleviate bull-whip effect can be extended to the use of convergence media which support high level of richness and more diverse mode of information. The impact and the future use of these emerging technologies and new coordination methodologies can be studies focusing on the effectiveness and efficiency of communication, building-up of trust, decision making accuracy, precision and flexibility, and the adoption of new innovative business and organizational processes.

It is often neglected that the adoption of a new technology is a very dynamic process, especially when it is related to a complex organizational setting such as organizational coordination. Adoption of a new technology triggers changes in the practice, structure, and strategy of organizations. While technology imperative perspective focuses on the impact that technology brings, organizational imperative perspective emphasize the impact of organization on technology. When a technology is assimilated into an organization or a society, the design, component, or use of the technology is selected and sometimes modified by the organization or the individual members of the organization. In addition, the changes in the behavior and mind of the members caused by the use of technology can, in turn, cause changes in the rules, processes, institutional systems, organizational values, and culture (Boudreau and Robey 2005). Such a dynamic and reciprocal complexity in a socio-technical interaction system is described as the reciprocal structuring process (Giddens 1984). Orlikowski's (1992) model of the duality of information technology, which is an application of Giddens' theory, can be a good ground for an analysis of the evolving use of emergent convergence technologies and their roles for organizational and supply network coordination.

The importance of coordination is gaining increased attention as the scope of coordination expands to supply network and new tools, technologies, and mechanisms are being suggested, experimented, and adopted widely. The emergence of new practices and technological landscape will help improving coordination among members of supply network. More research should be attempted to incorporate broader scope of coordination and new technological developments with an attempt to design and implement improved practices and mechanisms for future business coordination.

2.3 Task Characteristics and Research Hypotheses

This section summarizes the characteristics of tasks base on existing research. Base on the review, the relationships between the nature of task and the use of mobile office systems functions are drawn and hypothesized. Table 2. summarizes some selected research on the major dimensions of task characteristics which will be used in this research

2.3.1 Task Complexity

A task with high complexity is related to the use of deep knowledge and diverse information, requires large amount of experience, and is interrelated with many other tasks (Sheer and Chen, 2004). Task complexity is somewhat related to the analyzability of task. Analyzable tasks are related to predefined problems and well-organized formal procedure, rule, and information. On the other hand, unanalyzable tasks are irregular and differ across situation (Perrow 1986). When organizational environment is difficult to expect, tasks tend to be less analyzable and thus become complex. Tasks become complex when there are many factors to consider. However, in some cases a large portion of the factors are predetermined, while in other cases a large portion of the factors should be further determined and identified (Byström and Järvelin 1995; Byström 2002).

Blili et al. (1998) suggests that a high level of task complexity combined with high level of perceived importance of end user computing is related to high use and satisfaction of End User Computing. Sheer and Chen (2004) also verified that task complexity is an important independent variable in the selection of information processing medium. We hypothesize that a high level of task complexity will require more extensive use of mobile office systems.

Hypothesis 1: Task complexity is positively related to the use of mobile office functions.

Table 2 Selected research on the characteristics of task

Task characteristic	Suggestions and research contribution	Researchers
Task complexity	A task with high complexity is related to the use of deep knowledge and diverse information, requires large amount of experience, and is interrelated with many other tasks	Sheer and Chen (2004)
	A high level of task complexity combined with high level of perceived importance of end user computing is related to high use and satisfaction of End User Computing	Blili et al. (1998)
	Task complexity is somewhat related to the analyzability of task. Analyzable tasks are related to predefined problems and well-organized formal procedure, rule, and information. On the other hand, un analyzable tasks are irregular and differ across situation	Perrow (1986)
Task inter-dependence	Sharma and Yetton (2007) employed Pearce et al.'s measure of task interdependence to show the positive impact of task interdependence on the use of training system	Sharma and Yetton (2007), Pearce et al. (1992)
	Classified technical interdependence of organizational tasks into independent, sequential, and interactive tasks	Thompson (1967)
	High task interdependence increases the needs for coordination and cooperation among organizational members, and thus increases the level of task uncertainty and the needs for more information	Tushman and Nadler (1978)
	Task interdependence affect the level of information sharing using information systems and the level of individual performance	Gebauer (2006)
Task variability	Task variability is defined as the frequency of exceptional or unexpected new tasks to be performed that needs different or new approaches and methods	Sander and Courtney (1985)
	Measures task variability and includes such items as the amount of new tasks, routine tasks, and exceptional tasks	Van De Ven and Ferry (1980)
	The amount and type of information varies depending on the level of task variability and analyzability, resulting in the need for the use of different type of information media.	Daft and Lengel (1986)

(continued)

Table 2 (continued)

Task characteristic	Suggestions and research contribution	Researchers
Task mobility	Kakihara and Sorensen (2002) extend the concept of mobility beyond corporeal travel and suggest three dimensions of mobility: spatial mobility, temporal mobility, and contextual mobility	Kakihara and Sosensen (2002)
	Enhanced task mobility implies that users can receive required services anywhere, anytime	Grahan and Marvin (1996)
	Turban and King (2003) emphasized the importance of two dimensions in mobile environment; mobility and accessibility. They further suggest that location, individualization, ubiquity, and accessibility of products and services are the major sources of future value added	Turban and King (2003)
	Instant accessibility and connectivity implies information retrieval and exchange regardless of time and space, which is unique to Mobile Internet not available in any previous information media or systems	Durlache Research (2000)
	Identifies various benefits of increased mobility for the achievement of organizational goals	Basoele (2007)

2.3.2 Task Interdependence

Task interdependence is the degree by which organizational employees or department should depend on other organizational members to accomplish the goal of the task. When the interdependence of a task is low, employees can perform the task independently without various interactions with other members of the organization. Thompson (1967) classified technical interdependence of organizational tasks into independent, sequential, and interactive tasks. Independent task do not have dependence among tasks, while se sequentially interdependent task require the result of another task before the task is performed, requiring tight coordination and control among organizational tasks. Interactive task interdependence requires complicated inter-relationship among activities of several units to complete a task.

Tushman and Nadler (1978) suggests that high task interdependence increases the needs for coordination and cooperation among organizational members, and thus increases the level of task uncertainty and the needs for more and diverse information. Staple and Jarvenpaa (2000) showed that task interdependence affect the level of information sharing using information systems and the level of individual performance. Sharma and Yetton (2007) employed Pearce et al. (1992) measure of task interdependence to show the positive impact of task interdependence on the use of training system. We hypothesize that the high level of task interdependence is related to the high use of mobile office systems.

Hypothesis 2: Task interdependence is positively related to the use of mobile office functions.

2.3.3 Task Variability

Task variability is defined as the frequency of exceptional or unexpected new tasks to be performed that needs different or new approaches and methods (Sander and Courtney 1985; Perrow 1986). When a task can be performed with routine, repetitive operation and the routines can be expected without exceptional problems, the task is considered as low in task variability.

Daft and Lengel (1986) suggest that the amount and type of information varies depending on the level of task variability and analyzability, resulting in the need for the use of different type of information media. Task with high variability and low analyzability is considered to require computing tools which can provide broad scope of information in order to cope with unexpected situations.

In this research, we hypothesize that high task variability will require high level of the use of mobile office. We employed items from Van de Ven and Ferry (1980) to measure task variability and included such items as the amount of new tasks, routine tasks, and exceptional tasks.

Hypothesis 3: Task variability is positively related to the use of mobile office functions.

2.3.4 Task Mobility

Mobility represents the flow of people, resources, capital, and information (Swingedouw 1993). The widespread diffusion of Internet and wireless communication technologies triggered a radical change in the scope and meaning of mobility. Increased mobility is considered to broaden the scope of organizational communication, flexibility, and the efficiency of task processing, coordination, and control.

Mobile office applications are considered to provide increased freedom to organizational actors by helping them to overcome spatial and temporal limitations (Cherry 2007). Enhanced ability to optimize organizational resources is further considered to increase task productivity. Enhanced task mobility implies that users can receive required services anywhere and anytime (Grahan and Marvin 1996). Turban and King (2003) emphasized the importance of two dimensions in mobile environment; mobility and accessibility. They further suggest that location, individualization, ubiquity, and accessibility of products and services are the major sources of future value added.

Mobility can be considered as the key characteristics of mobile office environment as it determines the degree of efficient collection, application, and coordination of organizational resources. Basoele (2007) identifies various benefits of increased mobility for the achievement of organizational goals. Strategic benefit help companies improved real-time utilization of organizational resources, informational benefit enables convenient and fast exchange of accurate and useful information within and across an organization, and transactional benefit help reduce cost and innovate transactional relationships. In addition, mobility enables enterprise transformation so that new organizational structure and process can be explored.

Kakihara and Sorensen (2002) extend the concept of mobility beyond corporeal travel and suggest three dimensions of mobility: spatial mobility, temporal mobility, and contextual mobility. Spatial mobility is the movement of people, object, and symbols such as images and voices. Movement within on-line space is also included in spatial mobility. Temporal mobility stands for the changes in the concept and meaning of time due to improved operational speed and time saving. Here, the subject interpretation of time is more emphasized than the structural and objective measure of time. In this vein, the concept of *polychronicity*, which implies the performance of multiple tasks within a single time slot is related to the concept of temporal mobility. Contextual mobility implies contextual bounds of interaction in ensuring the dynamism of interaction among players through continuous monitoring, change, and intrusion.

This research views task mobility as the combination of spatial mobility as defined by Kakihara and Sorensen (2002) with instant accessibility and connectivity as used in previous research on mobile office systems. Instant accessibility and connectivity implies information retrieval and exchange regardless of time and space, which is unique to Mobile Internet not available in any previous information media or systems (Durlacher Research 2000).

Task mobility in this regard is a situation where task performance is accomplished along with changes in space. Task mobility, thus, may include at least two different types. In one type, a task is performed while moving outside of the company office. In another, a task is performed at a location outside of the company office after the movement or changes in space. In both situations, changes in the task processing space are observed. In a situation where a task is performed while moving, the task requirement may include heightened needs for fast information transfer and decision making via such general functions as e-mail, groupware, or information search. In a situation where a task is processed after moving to a certain location, the requirement tend to be a remote access to a specialized function of the corporate mobile office system rather than an urgent processing of a task. In both situations, we can hypothesize that the task mobility is expected to increase the need for heightened use of mobile office system.

Hypothesis 4: Task mobility is positively related to the high use of mobile office functions.

3 Research Method

3.1 Research Model

The purpose of this research is to examine the relationship between task characteristics and the use of mobile office in order to draw implications for appropriate design and use of mobile office systems. The nature information technology is considered to have a close relationship with task characteristics (Ling 1986) as information technology is used in an organization for the exchange of organizational knowledge and the coordination of organizational tasks (Orlikowski 1992; King and Xia 1997). For this reason, task characteristics should affect successful use of information technology in an organization. The research model of this study can be summarized as in Fig. 2.

3.2 Operational Definition of Variables

Task characteristics in this research are composed of task complexity, task interdependence, task variability, and task mobility. Task complexity means the level of diverse knowledge and information required for performing tasks and the needs for performing different types of tasks. Task complexity in this research is measured using the instrument developed by Blili et al. (1998). Task interdependence is the level of dependence on other departments, external organizations, or other organizational members in performing a given task. The instrument used by Sharma and Yetton (2007) and Pearce et al (1992) is also used in this research to measure task interdependence. Task variability is the amount of new or exceptional tasks, which require novel approaches and methods. Van De Ven and Ferry's (1980) measure for task variability is used in this research. Task mobility is

Fig. 2 Research model

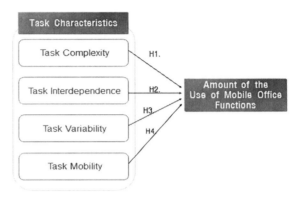

the level of spatial movement in performing a task. A new instrument for task mobility is developed and used in this research based on the research by Kakihara and Sosensen (2002) and Durlacher (2000).

Dependent variable is the use of mobile office in terms of the frequency and time length of the use of each function. Operational definitions of the research variables are summarized in Table 3.

3.3 Data Collection

Data were collected using a questionnaire, where all question items of the variables were designed using 5 point Likert-type scale. The questionnaire is administered to employees of Korean companies which adopted mobile office systems. The companies participated in the collection of research data include KT (Korea Telecom) in telecommunications industry, Seoul Metropolitan Railway Transit in public service industry which manage subway lines in Seoul, Samsung SDS in system integration and consultancy industry, Nokshipja in pharmaceutical industry, POSCO—the major player in steel industry, and SK in trading and energy industry. Key managers and executives were contacted so that the questionnaire be distributed to departments and functions which adopted mobile office applications. In addition, some questionnaires were also administered to individuals working in small and medium size companies, insurance resellers, and educational contents providers which use mobile office systems. Although the use of mobile office system is in its early stage, the sampling is considered to represent major part of different industries, companies, and functions that use this new technology.

The questionnaires were distributed out in different format depending on the situation and needs of respondents. Hard copies of the questionnaire were used

Table 3 Operational definitions of the research variables

Variables	Operational definition of variables	Researchers
Task complexity [1–6]	• diversity of task situation • complexity of task procedure/methods • number of task goals • task consistency • diversity of task performance measure	Blili et al. (1998)
Task inter-dependence [7–15]	• collaboration with other department • task processing related to other depts. • data/outcome dependence on other members or departments • level of independent task processing • task planning dependence • impact of other's task performance	Sharma and Yetton (2007) Pearce et al. (1992)
Task variability [16–18]	• amount of new tasks • level of repeated routine task • frequency of exceptional tasks	Sander and Courtney (1985) Van De Ven and Ferry (1980)
Task mobility [19–26]	• task processing while moving • location change for task processing • amount of time for movement • task processing outside of office • amount of system remote access • task space shared with other members	Kakihara and Sosensen (2002) Durlacher (2000)
Mobile office system use	• MOS use frequency [2.2.1–2.2.21] • MOS use time length [2.3.1–2.3.18]	Delone and McLean (1992)

along as well as soft copies using e-mail and corporate intranet as the medium. Total 239 questionnaires were collected. However, 26 responses were excluded in the first round of filtering as the responses were incomplete.

An initial analysis of the distribution of the data revealed a systematic bias in dependent variable toward low use (1 or 2 out of 5) as the use of mobile office system is still in its early stage. Since the purpose of the research is not to measure current state of adoption of the new technology, but to analyze the relationship between the independent variables (task characteristics) and the dependent variables (the use of mobile office systems), we decided to use a subsample of the data to represent different levels of use. The total data is divided into four quartiles: high use, moderately high use, moderately low us, and low use. Same number of data was randomly extracted from each quartile. Although this stratified subsampling severely reduced the number of data to be used, this procedure is considered required and appropriate to the purpose of the research. The final data set included 124 responses (31 responses from each quartile).

4 Results of Data Analysis

4.1 General Characteristics of the Sample

Total 124 questionnaires were analyzed using SPSS version 17.0. Analysis of the demographic characteristics of the respondents showed that percentage of respondents in the age of 31–35 was 25.6 %, 36–40 was 24.8 %, and 41–45 was 25.6 %, showing that ages between 31 and 45 comprises 76.0 % of the total. In terms of the industry of respondents, manufacturing was 10.4 %, construction 8 %, retail and transportation 7 %, insurance and finance 8.0 %, public organization 2.4 %, information and communication 46.4 %, medical and education 16.8 %, and other services comprised 7.2 % of the total sample representing diverse industries.

In terms of the department where the respondents belong, 64 % of the respondents belonged to sales and marketing, while 12.0 % belonged to planning and strategy, 11.2 % to production and technology support, and 11.2 % to IT and management information systems departments representing the extent and intensity of the adoption and use of mobile office systems. 27.2 % was low level employees, and middle level managers comprised 59.8 %, while 19.2 % was general managers and executives. 28.0 % of the respondents worked for the company for less than 3 years, while 20.8 % worked for 3–5 years, 15.2 % worked for 5–10 years, 22.4 % worked for 10–15 years, and 13.6 % worked for more than 15 years.

51.2 % of the respondents used mobile office systems based smart phones, while 48.8 % used mobile office systems based on notebook computers.

4.2 Test of Research Instruments

4.2.1 Test of Validity

Factor analyses based on principle component with varimax rotation was performed and factors with Eigen value over 1.0 were extracted. As for the dependent variable, Mobile Office usage, responses to the frequency (in 5 point scale) and the length of use (in 5 point scale) were multiplied to compute 18 usage variables.

As shown in Table 4, 4 factors were extracted from factor analysis. Factor 1 named as "information acquisition and exchange" included the use of internal data search, general data search, messenger, employee search, social network services, task scheduling, bulletin board and mobile on-line education. Factor 2 named as "specific task processing function" included the use of mobile SCM, mobile sales information system (SFA), mobile ERP, mobile field force automation (FFA) system, mobile BSC, mobile facility and safety management system (SYS). Factor 3 named as "customer and knowledge management function" included the use of mobile customer information management (CRM) system and mobile knowledge

Table 4 Factor analysis of the dependent variable (usage)

Items	Factors				Chronbach alpha
	1	2	3	4	
Internal data search	0.775	0.314	0.079	−0.049	0.866
Bulletin board	0.761	0.131	0.154	0.293	
Messenger	0.759	0.038	−0.234	−0.070	
Use_EDU	0.754	0.275	0.396	0.066	
Employee search	0.695	0.190	−0.224	0.384	
Data search	0.662	0.096	0.079	0.240	
Social network	0.658	−0.100	−0.012	−0.026	
Task scheduling	0.642	0.067	0.453	0.296	
Use_FFA	−0.014	0.824	0.296	0.006	0.837
Use_ERP	0.033	0.820	−0.110	0.262	
Use_SFA	0.001	0.751	0.158	0.072	
Use_SCM	0.167	0.750	0.416	−0.055	
Use_BSC	0.310	0.662	0.054	0.042	
Use_SYS	0.230	0.540	0.377	−0.217	
Use_CRM	−0.086	0.223	0.770	0.104	0.615
Use_KM	0.142	0.419	0.619	0.050	
E-approval	0.148	0.129	0.291	0.751	0.223
E-mail	0.439	−0.044	−0.391	0.552	

Principle component with Kaiser normalized varimax. 6 iterations were attempted

management (KM) system. Finally, factor 4 named as "general task processing function" included the use of electronic decision approval system and e-mail.

Factor analysis of 26 independent variable items including 6 task complexity items, 9 task interdependence items, 3 task variability items, and 8 task mobility items extracted 5 factors of task characteristics as shown in Table 5. 8 items were deleted by the analysis. Task mobility items were grouped into two factors and they are each named as "task mobility _accessibility while moving" and "task mobility _remote accessibility". 2 items were deleted in task complexity. Only 4 items out of 9 were saved for task interdependence factor.

4.2.2 Reliability Analysis

As for Cronbach's Alpha value of task complexity, interdependence, and mobility were all higher than 0.75, higher than then acceptable level of reliability. Among the task characteristics, Crohbach's Alpha of task variability was 0.577. However, as the items accepted showed logical consistency, we used this variable in the following analysis. We checked the reliability of the dependent variable although it is slightly different from typical perceptual construct. The reliability values of dependent variable were also acceptable except the last one, "general task processing function". For this reason, the last one is not used in the rest of analysis.

Table 5 Factor analysis of the independent variable (task characteristics)

Items	Factors					Chronbach alpha
	1	2	3	4	5	
Mobility1	0.880	−0.003	−0.029	0.198	0.093	0.923
Mobility2	0.870	0.097	0.084	0.044	−0.032	
Mobility3	0.863	0.005	−0.112	0.225	0.081	
Mobility4	0.851	0.077	−0.085	0.323	0.053	
Mobility5	0.738	0.006	0.008	0.286	−0.076	
Complexity4	0.108	0.774	0.054	−0.080	−0.143	0.782
Complexity3	−0.067	0.770	0.126	−0.060	−0.009	
Complexity2	0.078	0.749	−0.035	0.294	−0.095	
Complexity6	0.074	0.694	0.086	0.112	−0.309	
Interdependence7	0.102	−0.068	0.779	0.078	−0.309	0.769
Nterdependence8	0.184	−0.093	0.768	0.126	−0.215	
Interdependence5	−0.151	0.270	0.764	−0.081	0.127	
Interdependence6	−0.281	0.213	0.711	0.006	0.061	
Mobility7	0.282	0.083	0.088	0.834	−0.010	0.789
Mobility6	0.289	−0.045	0.136	0.725	−0.123	
Mobility8	0.448	0.192	−0.141	0.694	0.059	
Variability3	0.076	−0.156	−0.060	−0.032	0.831	0.577
Variability1	0.033	−0.250	−0.135	−0.028	0.692	

Principle component with Kaiser normalized varimax. 6 iterations were attempted

Fig. 3 Revised research model

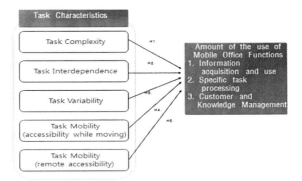

4.3 Revision of Research Model and Hypotheses

Based on the analysis of validity and reliability of the research variables, a slight modification of the research model and hypotheses is required. Dependent variable is divided into three groups as shown in Fig. 3. and Table 6. As for independent variables, task mobility is divided into two: task mobility _accessibility while moving and task mobility _remote accessibility.

Table 6 Revised research hypotheses

	Hypotheses
H1-1 ~ 3	Task complexity is positively related to the use of 1. Mobile information acquisition and exchange function 2. Mobile specific task processing function 3. Mobile customer and knowledge management function
H2-1 ~ 3	Task interdependence is positively related to the use of 1. Mobile information acquisition and exchange function 2. Mobile specific task processing function 3. Mobile customer and knowledge management function
H3-1 ~ 3	Task variability is positively related to the use of 1. Mobile information acquisition and exchange function 2. Mobile specific task processing function 3. Mobile customer and knowledge management function
H4-1 ~ 3	Task mobility _accessibility while moving is positively related to the use of 1. Mobile information acquisition and exchange function 2. Mobile specific task processing function 3. Mobile customer and knowledge management function
H5-1 ~ 3	Task mobility _remote accessibility is positively related to the use of 1. Mobile information acquisition and exchange function 2. Mobile specific task processing function 3. Mobile customer and knowledge management function

Table 7 Regression result on the use of information acquisition and exchange

Dependent var. (Information acquisition and exchange function)	B	t	Sig.	Acceptance
(constant)	0.567	0.162	0.871	
Task mobility-access while moving	0.613	3.286	0.001	Accept
Task complexity	0.701	1.239	0.218	Reject
Task interdependence	0.734	1.442	0.152	Reject
Task mobility-remote accessibility	−0.170	−0.437	0.663	Reject
Task variability	0.054	0.101	0.920	Reject

$R^2 = 0.118$

4.4 Test of Hypotheses

A series of Multiple Regression Analyses were performed to test the hypotheses presented by the research model.

4.4.1 Task Characteristics and the Use of Information Acquisition and Exchange Function

To test the relationship between task characteristics and the use of information acquisition and exchange function (H1-1, H2-1, H3-1, H4-1, H5-1), a multiple regressions were performed with the five independent variables. Table 7

Table 8 Regression result on the use of specific task processing function

Dependent Var. (specific task processing function)	B	t	Sig.	Acceptance
(constant)	−0.359	−0.244	0.807	
Task mobility-access while moving	0.643	80.191	0.000	Accept
Task complexity	−0.148	−0.620	0.536	Reject
Task interdependence	−0.269	−1.258	0.211	Reject
Task mobility-remote accessibility	0.637	3.901	0.000	Accept
Task variability	0.471	2.070	0.041	Accept

$R^2 = 0.478$

summarizes the results. The model explains 11.8 % of the variations of the dependent variable (sig.< 0.010). Only hypothesis 4-1 (mobility_ accessibility while moving) was accepted.

4.4.2 Task Characteristics and the Use of Specific Task Processing Function

A multiple regression to test the effect of task characteristics on the use of specific task processing function (H1-2, H2-2, H3-2, H4-2, H5-2) produced a result summarized in Table 8. The model explains 47.8 % of the variation (sig.< 0.000). Three hypotheses were accepted: hypothesis 3-2 (task variability; regression coefficient = 0.471, t value = 2.070, $p = 0.041$), hypothesis4-2 (task mobility _accessibility while moving; regression coefficient = 0.643, t value = 8.191, $p = 0.000$), hypothesis 5-2 (task mobility _remote accessibility; regression coefficient = 0.637, t value = 3.901, $p = 0.000$). Task complexity and interdependence did not affect the use of specific task processing function.

4.4.3 Task Characteristics and the Use of Customer and Knowledge Management Function

A multiple regression to test the effect of task characteristics on the use of customer and knowledge management function (H1-3, H2-3, H3-3, H4-3, H5-3) resulted in the acceptance of two hypotheses (H4-3 and H5-3) as summarized in Table 9. The model explains 35.7 % of the variation (sig. < 0.000). Mobility – accessibility while moving (H4-3) had regression coefficient of 0.403, t value of 2.903, and p of 0.004. Mobility _remote accessibility (H5-3) had regression coefficient of 1.254, t value of 4.332, and p of 0.000). Task complexity, task interdependence, and task variability did not affect the use of customer and knowledge management function.

Table 9 Regression result on the use of customer and knowledge management function

Dependent Var. (customer and knowledge management function)	B	t	Sig.	Acceptance
(constant)	2.226	0.854	0.395	
Task mobility-access while moving	0.403	2.903	0.004	Accept
Task complexity	0.611	1.448	0.150	Reject
Task interdependence	−1.772	−4.673	0.000	Reject
Task mobility-remote accessibility	1.254	4.332	0.000	Accept
Task variability	0.454	1.125	0.263	Reject

$R^2 = 0.357$

5 Case Study of the Use of Mobile Office

In this section the result of an exploratory case observation of the use of mobile office system is reported. We chose a public service organization known for its successful adoption and use of up-to-date mobile office system. SMRT (Seoul Metropolitan Railway Transit) is responsible for the operation of 4 subway lines in Seoul. This public organization, 100 % owned by the City of Seoul, applied the advanced smart phone-based mobile office system to the management of railway facilities. This case is unique in that it is an exception in several ways. First, it is a very early success example when the adoption of mobile office technology is still in its beginning stage. Second, it is a non-trivial application of the mobile office system. While most of the current use of mobile office system is used for marketing and sales functions, SMRT applied the technology to technical operation and services. Third, the adoption of such new technology in large public organization is highlighted as such organizations are typically known to be very conservative in adopting innovative approaches. We prepared the case by visiting the company and interviewing several important personnel including CIO, operational manager, and corporate planner.

5.1 Background of the Case Study

5.1.1 City Railway Services in Seoul

Seoul, the capital city of South Korea, is a modernized large-scale metropolitan city with the population of 11 million residences. Seoul has been the capital of Korea for the last 600 years. For this reason Seoul has full of historic monuments and palaces. The city of Seoul has been known as one of the fastest growing capital. Recently the

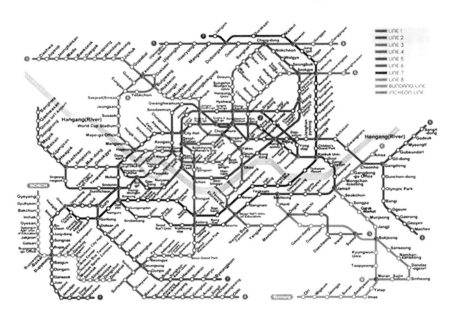

Fig. 4 Map of Seoul City Railway Lines

city received keen attention as it is chosen as one of the best city Asian people want to visit and as it is awarded the best e-government service provider to its citizen. The number of inbound visitors from abroad is also increasing rapidly.

Seoul has 8 completed lines of city railway, of which most of the line sections are subway lines moving under the ground. Two additional lines are under construction and 2 more lines are included in the master plan, making total 12 metropolitan railway lines by the end of the completion of the master plan. By now, 8 lines and part of line 9 and two city extension of Korea national railway make a complex and convenient coverage of the city of Seoul via fast railway network. As each train take passengers to almost every corner of the city and the train interval is maintained around 5 min, the city transportation in Seoul has become world-famous infrastructure. The metro system in Seoul is also known for its convenience, cleanliness, and modern technology (see Fig. 4 for the map).

The first subway line (line number 1, red line) in Seoul was built in 1974. Since then four lines were completed by 1985 based on the first stage city railway plan. The first four lines (red, green, orange, blue) are managed by Seoul Subway Company (renamed as Seoul Metro afterward). When the second stage city railway plan is completed, the city decided to establish a second company to manage the next 4 lines. There was an important reason for establishing a separate company instead of incorporating new lines into existing Seoul Metro. By making two separate companies and evaluating their quality of services periodically, the city could introduce the competing mind into public services. The two companies, through competition, are expected to compete to gain high reputation in their service provision and to maintain organizational tension toward innovation and improvement.

5.1.2 Seoul Metropolitan Transit Railway (SMRT) Company Overview

Seoul Metropolitan Railway Transit (SMRT) Company is a government-owned public company owned 100 % by the City of Seoul. SMRT was established in 1994 in order to manage city railway services for lines number 5, 6, 7, and 8.

SMRT manages 148 stations and 6 large-scale maintenance centers. The company operates 1,560 coach compartments and 152 km of railway lines in Seoul carry 3,390,000 passengers per day. Line 5 operates 608 compartments (8 × 76 coaches) carrying 1,160,000 passengers per day, line 6 operates 328 compartments (8 × 41 coaches) carrying 650,000 passengers per day, line 7 operates 504 compartments (8 × 63 coaches) carrying 1,270,000 passengers per day, and line 8 operates 120 compartments (6 × 20 coaches) carrying 310,000 passengers per day. Daily revenue from fare collection is about 1.3 billion KRW.

SMRT ranked as number 1 in the management evaluation among all public service companies belong to the Ministry of Government Administration and Home Affairs for 4 consecutive years from 2005 to 2008. SMRT also ranked top in 2008 in Integrated Railway Safety Review performed by the Ministry of Land, Transport and Maritime Affairs among all railway operators in Korea.

5.2 Adoption of Mobile Office System at SMRT

5.2.1 Business Practice of SMRT During 1994–2009

SMRT has about 30,000 Major facilities. List of the whole facility include over one million items scattered all around the city. For this reason employees of SMRT keep move around the city to locate and manage the facilities of responsibility.

Since the birth of SMRT in 1994 the task scheduling, assignment, orders, and reporting was processed manually up until 2004. Every morning each employee should go to the company headquarter, confirm the task order of the day, and receive work order sheet. They carry the work-order to the location of the facility, process the task assigned, and complete the work-order sheet manually. After returning back to the office, they again should fill-up the completion report about the task they performed.

Such manual work process produced enormous amount of paper documents and the company should devote massive amount of time and effort to manage, transport, and store the documents. Employees had to spend 20 % of their time on the street to move back and forth from office and facility in addition to commuting. In addition 30 % of employee time devoted to create and manage administrative documents and to participate in meetings. For this reason only 50 % of their time was used to take care of the actual tasks of facility check-ups, maintenance, adjustments, and operations.

After computerized reporting system was adopted in 2006, employees could be freed from the manual creation of work-completion report at the end of the day.

The keyed in the report contents about the work they completed in each day. The accuracy and usability of data has increased. However, the time spend on the street was same as before as the other processes including picking up the paper-based work-order sheet were remained unchanged. Still 20 % of employee time was used for moving back and forth and 25 % of the time was used for administrative chore. In addition, people waited on a line to enter the report as the peak load is concentrated toward the end of the day.

5.2.2 Mobile Office System Development Project at SMRT

Mobile Office System is considered to have the potential to innovate business practices as the infrastructure, application, and terminal equipment becomes reliable and smart. Korea is well known in the quality of telecommunication infrastructure. Since 1995, the Korean government drove the establishment and adoption of broadband backbone through Giga-Internet project, high-speed network project as well as the adoption of 'Wibro' mobile infrastructure and smart applications. The introduction of smart phone such as iPhone opened up the potential to optimize the use of such telecommunication infrastructure. Smart phones provide improved flexibility and applicability compared to existing mobile support environment such as PDAs and laptops.

The top management initiated the radical changes in business process to reduce non-task waste of employee time using advances in technological environment. He decided the development of mobile office system which can economize on the use of smart phones. Initial skepticism on the social effect, technical functionality, speed, fear for being connected and monitored were expressed the voice of labor union. Close communication about the potential problems and solutions with the employees was helpful in pursuing the project in a cooperative atmosphere.

The CIO of SMRT decided to develop the application systems in-house as he did not want to be overly dependent on external services in future changes and developments of the system. Fast experience of hiring several external developers in the development of separate information systems might affect this decision. With the help of KT(Korea Telecom), the MOS infrastructure service provider, they started the development of internal service network, inter-connection with existing legacy information, and the development of mobile applications.

In this vein, they re-organized IT Division by combining existing three separate departments: IT planning, system development, and technology analysis. They strengthened technical capability by recruiting more engineers, emphasizing updated technical training for existing IT members, and facilitating the sharing of development results, experiences, knowledge, and skill. They focused on the development of mobile office system applications, technology, and services best fit to the situation of the company and user groups.

5.3 Characteristics of the Mobile Office System of SMRT

By combining existing IS applications (such as engineering systems, electronic engineering and product design management system, and facility management system) and wireless personal media, SMRT could successfully develop a mobile task-supporting environment, first of its kind in the world as they mentioned, that help the management of subway lines real-time without the restriction of time and space. They named the system as ST&F (SMRT Talk and Flash).

Thanks to the adoption of ST&F, employees now do not have to commute to the company headquarter office in the morning. Employees receive work-order via their individual smart phones before they leave home. They commute directly to the location assigned for planned and regular check-ups or to the location of facility with problem report. After completing the task the employees report the completion of the task real-time using the applications in their smart phones.

The top menu of ST&F system includes Problem Reporting, Company Announcements, Approval of Railway Tasks, Operation Procedure Guide, and Barcode Inquiry.

5.3.1 ST&F Problem Reporting System

Previously, problem reporting was a task assigned only to technicians in charge of facility check-up. After the mobile office system put in place, any member of SMRT can file the problem report wherever and whenever they find a problem in equipment and facilities while commuting or while working around. Immediately after the problem report is forwarded, a responsible and qualified technician closest to the spot while moving around is assigned the repairing and maintenance job. The problem is fixed real-time and the result of resolution is reported.

There are three different methods of problem reporting: the use of ST&F barcode picture capturing, the use of company private phone line, and the use of SMS or public phone by citizen. When the ST&F is used, one use smart phone to take the picture of QR code attached in each facility or equipment. Then the facility or equipment information is retrieved and a menu to report a problem pops up so that the reporting can be completed on the spot (refer to Fig. 5).

5.3.2 ST&F Barcode Processing System

ST&F Barcode Processing System is linked to the corporate facility management system so that problem reporting, part history management, and problem resolution result reporting can be completed through one integrated interface. Although the reporter does not have sufficient knowledge on the facility of concern, the

Fig. 5 Alternative procedures of SMRT problem reporting

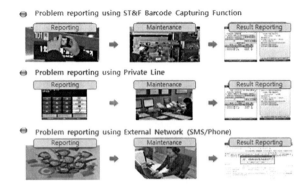

Fig. 6 Problem reporting using ST&F barcode capturing function

Fig. 7 ST&F part history management system

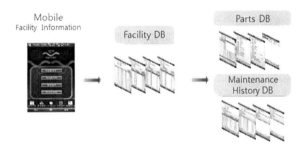

system help the user find key information so that any authorized employee can report a problem or the result of task completion (refer to Fig. 6).

5.3.3 ST&F Part History Manager

ST&F Part History Management system helps employees to search and review the current status as well as the detailed history of the maintenance of all equipment, facilities, and parts as a group or by individual items with just one simple touch of a button of their smart phones (refer to Fig. 7).

5.3.4 ST&F Operating Procedure Guide System

ST&F Operating Procedure Guide System provide SOP (Standard Operating Procedures) and response methods to the occurrence of such emergency situation as fire, railway delay, explosion or earthquake. SOP and response method include step-by-step response procedures to crises for all types of tasks such as integrated controlling, customer services, driving, coach handling, and engineering. It includes action guidelines at the spot, facilities and equipment handling guidelines, corporate rules by roles, as well as the methods for CPR (Cardiopulmonary Resuscitation).

5.4 Effect of the Adoption of Mobile Office System at SMRT

After the adoption of ST&F system, the employees do not have to commute to the headquarter office in the morning. All the employees received the daily task assignment via their smart phones. They can directly go to the location appropriate to the completion of the mission such as periodic check-ups and problem handling. After the completion of the mission, they report the results immediately and directly to the central office.

The new practice reduced the time for moving back and forth to 10 % of their working time from previous 20 % (a 100 % improvement). The time used for paper works and administration chore also reduced to 10 % of their working time from previous 30 % (a 200 % improvement) on the average. The employees could use 80 % of their time to concentrate on the completion of assigned task. The effect of this improvement resulted in the heightened efficiency of the use of human resources and the heightened level of railway safety.

The response time between problem reporting and the completion of problem fixing has also reduced dramatically to 20 min from 2 h in previous practice. The ST&F Barcode Recognition helped every employee to report a problem they found and simple fix result without detailed technical knowledge, virtually every employee of SMRT turned into facility managers. The effect turned out as the increase of preventive maintenance and the reduction of defect-occurrence rate by 40 % compared to pre-adoption period.

In addition, the use of ST&F Part History Manager and Operating Procedure Guide systems helped standardize the performance reducing the discrepancy in the quality of task results between novices and skilled experts. This improvement increased the overall level of confidence of employees in performing their tasks.

The company reports that the total monetary benefit from the ST&F system is expected to be 220 billion KRW (about 200 million USD), which include the annual reduction of operating costs (28.4 billion KRW) and revenues from new business services. Since the total investment into ST&F was 10.2 billion KRW, the benefit is way far surpassing the investment.

The system also facilitated the enhancement of the reputation of the company. As the success of ST&F system of SMRT drew attention among industry professionals, experts from Canada, Singapore, and China visited SMRT for a benchmarking. Based on the confidence in their technological achievement, SMRT is pursuing the commercialization of the system to make it a new business to create extra revenue from the provision of software and consulting services to domestic as well international railway operators.

6 Conclusion

Technological application based on Internet and wireless network provides both economic benefits and new business opportunities. As the level of uncertainty from market environments and corresponding agility of companies experience rapid changes, the importance of smart responses and improved mobility is increasing. Mobile office systems is a technological solution which incorporate both advanced smart and mobile attribute of modern information technology. For this reason increasing number of companies show interests in adopting this technological system.

The survey research focused on the factors related to the successful adoption and use of mobile office systems. Especially, we focused on the match between the characteristics of organizational tasks and the use of mobile office systems from the perspective of task-technology fit.

First of all, the result of the research showed that the level of task mobility is positively related to the use of both general and specialized functions of mobile office systems. Second, the execution of tasks with high level of interdependence with other tasks, departments, and external organizations is correlated to the use of specialized functions such as mobile-based FFA, SFA, and ERP of the mobile office system. Third, tasks with high level of variability where new procedures and exceptional requirements keep emerging tend to need the use of specialized mobile office functions.

The result implies that companies that perform tasks with high level of uncertainty and interdependence should focus on the active adoption and use of specialized functions of mobile office. On the other hand, organizations which rely on a lot of internal communications and tasks with high level of mobility need to adopt a system with well-developed general mobile office functions.

Additional analyses focusing on the differences of the use of mobile office by department and the level of hierarchy showed some interesting evidences. For example, sales department used general functions more extensively than specialized functions compared to other departments. This result is consistent with the major results of the analysis of hypotheses in that tasks of sales department rely more on mobility than other departments.

The result of this research implies that understanding the nature of tasks of a company should precede the design and adoption of different functions of mobile office systems. Such customized adoption strategy will help calibrate the investments into mobile office systems so that the effects and benefits from investments can be optimized.

Most of all, task mobility is found to be the most influential attribute of task in the use of mobile office system. This result implies that when a mobile office system is introduced into an organization, high priority should be given to users who perform tasks with high level of mobility. We may also expect that future organizations will use more tasks using mobile office systems, and it implies the level of overall mobility of organizations will also increase by way of using more participative and collaborative strategies and end up to creating new organizational culture of communication, information sharing, and decision making.

Smartness and mobility has become the strategic necessity of today's corporate world. Mobile office system successfully incorporates both of these two attributes. However, consideration of the specifics and contingencies of organizational and task needs should be made for desired results. The case of SMRT shows how business needs and task characteristics fit to the use of technology.

They could successfully innovate the speed and quality of public services scattered around the city by way of using advances in high-speed mobile infrastructure, applications, and equipment to support employees in high level of mobility. Based on the understanding that the new technology is going to be of practical and effective support of their tasks, internal members of the company actively pursued the design and development of new systems rather than simply hiring and relying on external technology vendors.

One learning from the case is that the members of a user company, who understand the nature of the task should take initiative in developing a noble technology. In addition, the case of SMRT shows that the mobile office system can be applied and extended to various business areas such as facility management and maintenance beyond such typical uses as sales and marketing support. In this sense, the underlying characteristics of task of greater concern than the functional definitions of a task for improved coordination.

I would like to suggest the concept of 'convergent coordination'. Convergent coordination is a strategy for organizational coordination based on the use of converged media. Converged media is a technology which combines audio-based media, text-based media, and video-based media. Such convergence media has the potential to provide enhanced level of mobility and richness (Daft and Lengel 1986). Achieving high level of convergent coordination is believed to be the strategic necessity for the sustainable success of future organizations.

Future research can be extended at least in three directions. First, the logic of convergent coordination can be empirically verified and refined with more extensive sample of organizations in different industries. Second, a more detailed and practical guidelines for convergent coordination can be made through a careful analysis of the task processes in different nature. Third, as the accumulation of the new technology is expected to lead structural changes in the industrial ecosystem, the changes in the web of business relationship structure should be examined to help understand the nature of paradigmatic changes in the future of our economy.

References

Alavi, M., & Leidner, D. E. (1999). Knowledge management systems: issues, challenges, and benefits, *Communication of the Association for Information Systems, 1*(2).

Argyres, N. (1999). The impact of information technology on coordination: Evidence from the B-2 'Stealth' Bomber. *Organization Science, 10*(2), 162–180.

Arshinder, A. K., & Deshmukh, S. G. (2008). Supply chain coordination: Perspectives, empirical studies, and research directions. *International Journal of Production Economics, 115*(2), 316–335.

Astley W. G., & Van de Ven, A. H. (1983). Central perspectives and debates in organization theory. *Administrative Science Quarterly, 28*, 245–273.

Ballou, R. H., Gilbert, S. M., & Mukherjee, A. (2000). New managerial challenges from supply chain opportunities. *Industrial Marketing Management, 29*(1), 7–18.

Barratt, M. (2004). Understanding the meaning of collaboration in the supply chain. *Supply Chain Management: An International Journal, 9*(1), 30–42.

Basole, R. (2007). Strategic planning for enterprise mobility: A readiness-centric approach. association for information system proceeding.

Beulen, E., & Streng, R. (2002). The impact of online mobile office applications on the effectiveness and efficiency of mobile workers behavior: A field experiment in the IT services sector. *Proceedings of 23rd ICIS Conference.*

Blili, S., Raymond, L., & Rivard, S. (1998). Impact of task uncertainty, end user involvement and competence on the success of end user computing. *Information Management, 33*, 137–153.

Bonabeau, E. (2003). Don't trust your gut. *Harvard Business Review, 116–123.*

Boudreau, M. C., & Robey, D. (2005). Enacting integrated information technology: A human agency perspective. *Organization Science, 16*(1), 3–18.

Broadcasting and Communications Council of Korea (2010). National Plan to Roll-out Wireless Internet for Advanced Smart Mobile Society 4.

Byström, K. (2002). Information and information sources in tasks of varying complexity. *Journal of the American Society for Information Science and Technology, 53*(7), 581–591.

Byström, K., & Järvelin, K. (1995). Task complexity affects information seeking and use. *Information Processing and Management, 31*(2), 191–213.

Cachon, G. P., & Fisher, M. (2000). Supply chain inventory management and the value of shared information. *Management Science, 46*(8), 1032–1048.

Cherry, C. (2007). *The telephone system: Creator of mobility and social change. The social impact of the telephone.* Cambridge: The MIT Press.

Cho, N., Li, G., & Su, C. (2007). Am empirical study on the effect of individual factors on knowledge sharing by knowledge type. *Journal of Global Business and Technology, 3*(2), 1–15.

Daft, R. L., & Lengel, R. H. (1986). Organizational information requirements, media richness, and structural design. *Management Science, 32*(5), 554–571.

Daft, R. L., Lengel, R. H., & Trevino, L. K. (1987). Message equivocality, media selection and manager performance: Implications for information systems. *MIS Quarterly, 11*(3), 355–366.

Delone, W. H., & McLean, E. R. (1992). Information systems success: The quest for the dependent variable. *Information Systems Research, 3*(1), 60–95.

Ding, D., & Chen, J. (2008). Coordinating three level supply chain with flexible returns policies. *Omega, 36*(4), 865–876.

Durlacher Research Ltd, Mobile Commerce Report (2000).

Faraj, S. A., & Xiao, Y. (2006). Coordination in fast-response organizations. *Management Science, 52*(8), 1155–1169.

Galbraith, J. R. (1977). *Organization design.* Reading: Addison-Wesley.

Gebauer, J., & Shaw, M. (2004). Usage and impact of mobile business application-an assessment based on the concepts of task/technology fit. *Proceedings of the Tenth Americas Conference on Information Systems.* New York, August, 2004.

Gebauer J. (2006) Task-technology fit for mobile information systems. Available at. http://www. business.uiuc.edu/ Working_Papers/papers/06-0107.

Ghani, J. A. (1992). Task uncertainty and the use of computer technology. *Information and Management, 12*(2), 69–76.

Giddens, A. (1984). *The constitution of society: Outline of the theory of structure.* Berkeley: University of California Press.

Gittell, J. H., & Weiss, L. (2004). Coordination networks within and across organizations: A multi-level framework, *Journal of Management Studies, 41*(1), 127–153.

Goodhue, D., & Thompson, R. L. (1995). Task-technology fit and individual performance. *MIS Quarterly, 19*(2), 213–236.

Gordon, L. A., & Miller, D. (1976). A contingency framework for the design of accounting information systems. *Accounting, Organizations and Society, 1*(1), 59–69.

Graham, S., & Marvin, S. (1996). *Telecommunications and the city: Electronic spaces.* Urban Places, London: Routledge.

Hoyt, J., & Huq, F. (2000). From arms-length to collaborative relationships in the supply chain: An evolutionary process. *International Journal of Physical Distribution and Logistics Management, 30*(9), 750–764.

Kakihara, M., & Sorensen, C. (2002). Mobility: An extended perspective. *HICSS Proceeding,* 2002.

Kanawattanachai, P., & Yoo, Y. (2007). The impact of knowledge coordination on virtual team performance over time. *MIS Quarterly, 31*(4), 783–808.

King, R. C., & Xia, W. (1997). Media appropriateness: Effects of experience on communication media choice. *Decision Science, 28*(4), 877–910.

Kirs, P. J., Sanders, G. L., Ceveny, R. P., & Robey, D. (1989). An Experimental validation of the Gorry and Scott Morton Framework. *MIS Quarterly, 13*(2), 183–197

KT Economics Research Center (2010). *Economy effect of mobile office,* March 2010.

Ling, T. P. (1986). Critical success factors of decision support systems: An experimental study. *Database, 17*(2), 3–16.

Majchzak, A., Rice, R. E., Malhotra, A., King, N., & Ba, S. (2000). Technology adaptation: The case of a computer-supported inter-organizational virtual team. *MIS Quarterly, 24*(4), 569–600.

Malone, T., & Crowston, K. (1994). The interdisciplinary study of coordination. *ACM Computing Surveys, 26*(1), 87–119.

Melnyk, S. A., Davis, E. W., Spekman, R. E., & Sandor, J. (2010). Outcome-driven supply chains. *MIT Sloan Management Review, 51*(2), 33–38.

Nadler, D. A., & Tushman, M. L. (1998). *Competing by design: The power of organizational architecture.* Oxford: Oxford University Press.

Orlikowski, W. J. (1992). The duality of technology: Rethinking the concept of technology in organizations. *Organization Science, 3*(3), 398–427.

Osborn, R. N., & Hunt, J. G. (1974). Environment and organizational effectiveness. *Administrative Science Quarterly, 19*(2), 231–246.

Pearce. J. L., Sommer, S. M., Morris, A., & Frideger, M. (1992). *A configurational approach to interpersonal relations: Profiles of workplace social relations and task interdependence, GSM#OB92015 1992.* Irvine: University of California.

Perrow. (1986). *Complex organizations a critical essay.* New York: Random House.

Rice, R. E. (1992). Task analyzability, use of new media, and effectiveness: A multi-site exploration of media richness. *Organization Science, 3*(4), 475–500.

Samsung Economics Research Institute (2010). Smart phone opens a new future, 3 Feb 2010.

Sanders, G. L., & Courtney, J. F. (1985). A field study of organizational factors influencing DSS success. *MIS Quarterly, 9*(1), 77–89.

Sharma. R., & Yetton, P. (2007). The contingent effects of training, technical complexity and task interdependence on successful information systems implementation. *MIS Quarterly, 31*(2), 219–238.

Sheer, V. C., & Chen, L. (2004). Improving media richness theory: A study of interaction goals, message valence, and task complexity in manager-subordinate communication. *Management Communication Quarterly, 11*(1).

Staples, D. S., & Jarvenpaa, S. L. (2000). Using Electronic Media for Information Sharing Activities: A replication and extension (pp.117–133). *Proceedings of the 21st ICIS*, December 10–13.

Swingedouw, E. (1993). Communication, mobility and the struggle for power over space, In G. Gianopoulos & A. Gillespie (Eds.), *Transportation and communication innovation in Europe*.

Thompson, J. D. (1967). *Organization in action*. New York: McGraw-Hill.

Tichy, N. (1983). *Managing strategic change: Technical, Political and cultural dynamics*. New York: Wiley.

Turban, E., & King, D. (2003). *Introduction to E-commerce*. New Jersey: Prentice Hall.

Tushman, M. L., & Nadler, D. A. (1978). Information processing as an integrating concept in organization design. *The Academy of Management Review, 3*(3), 613–624.

Van de Ven, A. H., & Ferry, D. L. (1980). *Measuring and assessing organizations*. New York: Wiley.

Weill, P., & Olson, M. (1989). An assessment of contingency theory. *Journal of Information System, 6*(1), 59–86.

Yasai-Ardekani, M. (1986). Structural adaptations to environments. *Academy of Management Review, 11*(1), 9–21.

Zhou, H., & W. C. Benton Jr. (2007). Supply chain practice and information sharing. *Journal of Operations Management, 25*, 1348–1365.

Printed by Printforce, the Netherlands